921
FRA

C.l

Parker, Steve.

Benjamin Franklin and
electricity.

34880030013291

$18.55

921
FRA

C.l

Parker, Steve.

Benjamin Franklin
and
electricity.

34880030013291

$18.55

DATE	BORROWER'S NAME	
	S.J.	306
	Mat Morales	205

BAKER & TAYLOR

Science Discoveries

BENJAMIN

FRANKLIN

and Electricity

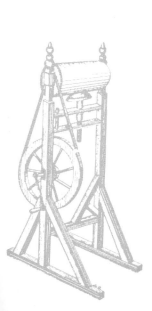

Steve Parker

Chelsea House Publishers
Philadelphia

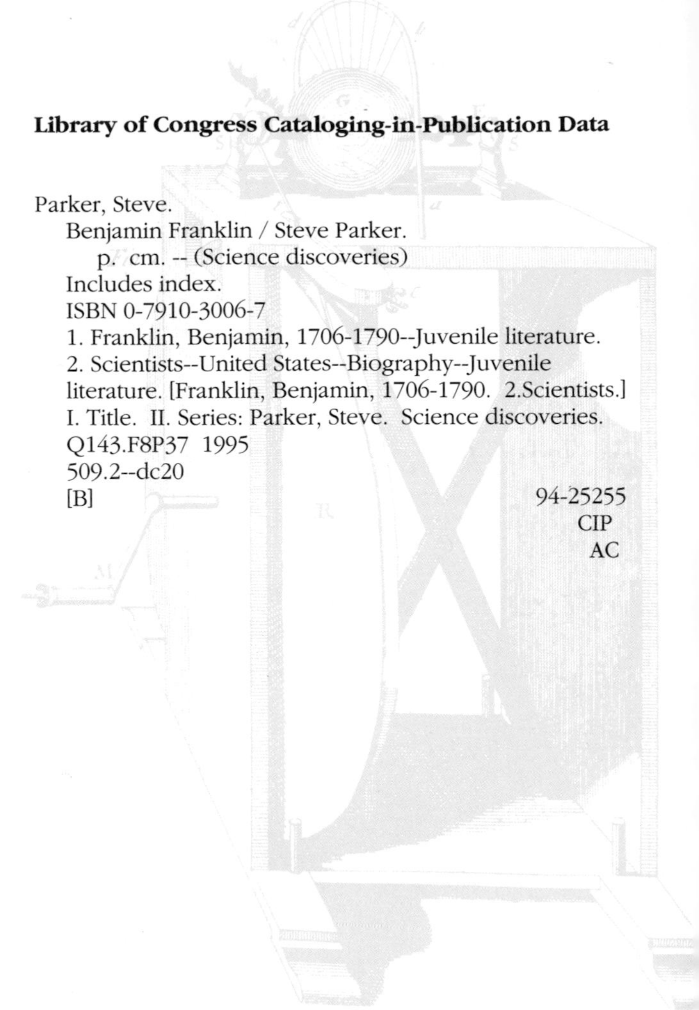

This edition © Chelsea House Publishers 1995,
a subsidiary of Haights Cross Communications.

First published in Great Britain in 1995 by
Belitha Press Limited

Copyright © Belitha Press Limited 1995
Text © Steve Parker 1995

Illustrations/photographs © in this format by Belitha
Press Limited 1995

5 7 9 8 6 4
ISBN 0-7910-3006-7

Printed in Malaysia

Photographic credits:
Bridgeman Art Library: Title page private collection, 8
    top Lincolnshire County Council, Usher Gallery
    Lincoln, 19 bottom Library Company of Philidelphia
    Pennsylvania, 20 center Dr Williams' Library
E.T. Archive: 14 bottom
Mary Evans Picture Library: 6 bottom left and bottom
    right, 7 top, 8 bottom right, 9 bottom left, 10 top, 18
    19 top, 20 top, 21 right, 25 bottom, 26 bottom
Image Select: 15 top
The Mansell Collection: 6 center, 16 both, 17 top
Peter Newark's American Pictures: 4 top, 5 top, 8
    bottom left, 9 top and bottom right, 10 both, 11
    both, 13 both, 14 top, 24 top, 25 top, 27 top right
Photri Inc: 5 bottom, 24 bottom, 27 top left
The Royal Society, London: 22 top, 23 left
Science Photo Library: 4 bottom Manfred Kage, 15
    bottom left Sinclair Stammers, 15 bottom right
    Vaughan Fleming, 17 bottom David Taylor, 21 left
    Nelson Medina, 26 top Peter Menzel

Cover images provided by Image Select, Mary Evans
Picture Library, The Mansell Collection and Peter
Newark's Western Americana

Illustrations by Tony Smith
Diagrams by Peter Bull

Editor: Struan Reid
Design: Cooper Wilson Limited
Picture research: Juliet Duff
Specialist adviser: Marina Benjamin

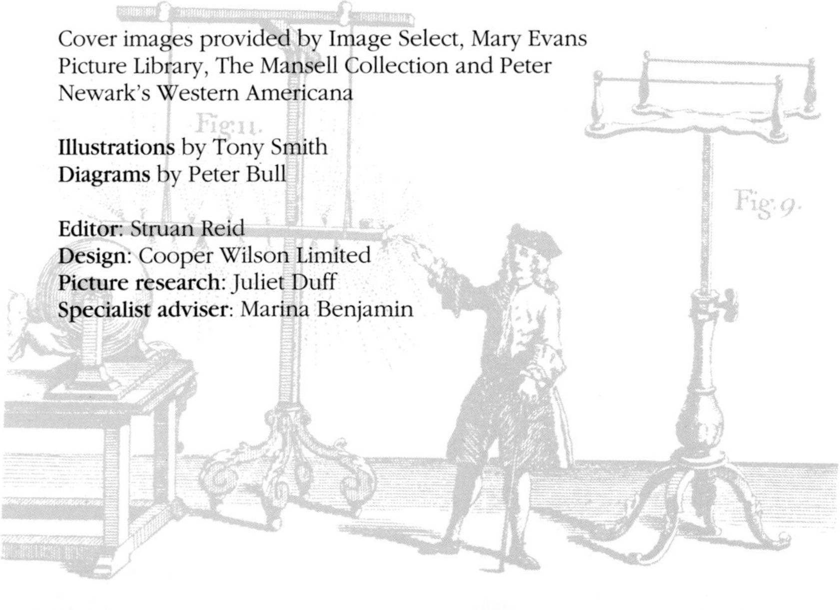

Library of Congress Cataloging-in-Publication Data

Parker, Steve.
    Benjamin Franklin / Steve Parker.
        p. cm. -- (Science discoveries)
    Includes index.
    ISBN 0-7910-3006-7
    1. Franklin, Benjamin, 1706-1790--Juvenile literature.
    2. Scientists--United States--Biography--Juvenile
    literature. [Franklin, Benjamin, 1706-1790. 2.Scientists.]
    I. Title. II. Series: Parker, Steve. Science discoveries.
    Q143.F8P37 1995
    509.2--dc20
    [B]   94-25255
                                                CIP
                                                AC

Fig. 11.

Fig. 9.

Contents

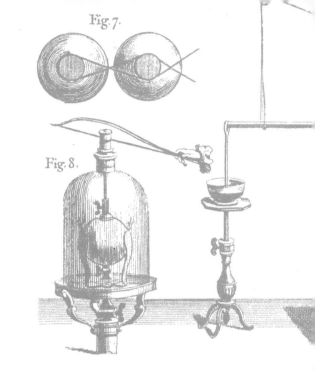

Introduction

The electrical **cell**, or "**battery**," was invented in 1800 by an Italian professor of physics named Alessandro Volta. For the first time a steady supply of flowing electricity became available – what we would call an **electric current**. Before 1800, a number of people had experimented with electricity and its effects and used it in certain machines and also toys. But the electricity was in a much less controllable form and did not flow steadily. This form is usually called static electricity.

In the century before Volta, many scientists studied static electricity. One of the most important was Benjamin Franklin. He carried out experiments and increased the understanding of electrical effects. He was also the first person to use the now-familiar terms *positive* and *negative* in electricity.

Franklin did much more in science. He devised several inventions, such as the lightning conductor, bifocal spectacles, a musical instrument, and a more efficient design of a stove or fireplace. He studied the oceans and their water currents. He was also a successful printer and writer. In addition, he was a highly respected and important political figure in America and Europe during the time the United States became an independent nation.

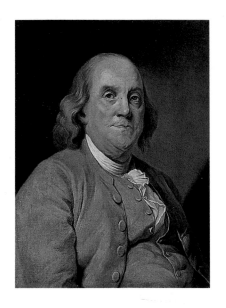

Benjamin Franklin, "America's first famous scientist," in his later years. By this time he was a respected figure in a newly independent nation.

Leaf with electromagnetic discharge. Franklin's most famous experiments were with electricity.

Chapter One
The Early Years

In the early 1700s, the United States of America did not exist. The lands that now make up the northeast states of America were a collection of different **colonies** under the control of the far-off government in Britain. There were three main cities along the east coast: Boston, New York, and Philadelphia. The lands to the west of the Appalachian Mountains were inhabited by **Native Americans**. Few Europeans had dared to venture there yet.

Benjamin Franklin was born in Boston, in the colony of Massachusetts, on January 17, 1706. Boston was a fast-growing port. Many **immigrants** arrived there, mainly from Europe, hoping for a better life in the new colonies of North America.

One of these immigrants had been Benjamin's father, Josiah Franklin. He had arrived in Boston in 1683 with his wife, Anne, and their three children. They established a business and a home and had four more children.

Map of colonial North America in 1775. At this time the European settlements were restricted to the eastern coast. Not until the beginning of the next century did people explore the lands to the west of the Appalachian Mountains.

Boston in about 1750. The city was an important port and commercial center.

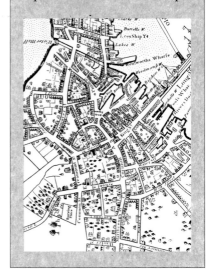

A candle-making business in the early 18th century, showing the various stages involved.

Many Mouths to Feed

Anne died in 1689 and Josiah married again. His second wife was Abiah, an American-born daughter of the Folger family from Nantucket Island. Josiah and Abiah had ten children together. Benjamin was the youngest of his father's seventeen children.

Young Ben grew up in a busy household filled with the smells of simmering candle tallow (animal fat) and soap. Before Josiah left for America, he had lived in Banbury, Oxfordshire, and had worked as a textile dyer. In Boston, he changed to making candles and soaps and set up a shop to earn a living.

Franklin Family Life

Josiah was an educated man compared to many other tradespeople. He encouraged Ben to read and write. By the age of seven, Ben gained an appetite for books and languages that would continue through his life. He admired his father's solid judgment and his mother's goodness and virtue. These were to influence him for the rest of his long life.

The house on Milk Street in Boston where Ben Franklin was born.

A Brief Schooling

At the age of eight, Ben went to grammar school. His father wanted him to become a church minister. But the school was costly, and the Franklin family was not rich. After a year, young Ben was transferred to another school where he spent two years. That was the end of his schooling. Like George Washington, Ben Franklin was largely self-taught. He then began work in his father's business.

A Start in Printing

Josiah took his son around Boston, hoping that he would take up one of the many trades or crafts practiced in the city. But "bookish Ben" was more interested in reading and writing.

In 1718, one of Ben's brothers, James, returned from London, England, where he had learned the printing trade. James set up a printing business in Boston, on a road later called Franklin Avenue. Ben, now 12 years old, became his **apprentice**. So began the first main career of his long and varied life.

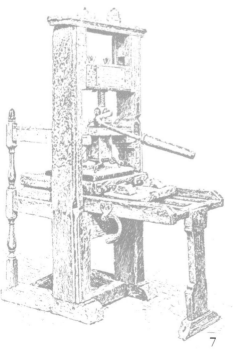

A printing works in Europe in the 18th century. Franklin's brother James learned the business in London and then set up his own printing works in Boston.

7

Chapter Two
Getting Established

The young Benjamin Franklin enjoyed the reading and writing that went with his apprenticeship as a printer. He especially enjoyed reading Joseph Addison's essays in the English *Spectator* magazine.

However, the conditions of work were hard, with long hours. Brother James was a strict employer, and the training was due to last nine years.

Stirring Up Trouble

In 1721, James Franklin founded his own weekly **broadsheet**, called the *New England Courant*. Its articles often criticized politicians and religious leaders in the Boston area for doing nothing to ease the hardships of ordinary people.

Benjamin became interested in these views and wrote some articles for the paper. He was not really allowed to do this as he was only an apprentice. In 1722, James was imprisoned for a month because of the views expressed in the paper. Ben took over as editor and learned about printing and publishing.

Joseph Addison (1672-1719), politician and writer who advocated moderation in life.

A page from the Spectator *magazine, at the time Addison was writing for it.*

Franklin admired English writer Daniel Defoe, punished for his political views.

To Philadelphia

Ben later quarreled with his brother James and decided to leave home. He traveled from Boston to New York and eventually to Philadelphia, Pennsylvania. He arrived with no job, almost no money, and only a loaf of bread to eat.

Philadelphia was to be Franklin's home for much of the rest of his life. He soon found a job in printing and courted Deborah Read, the daughter of his first landlady.

A year later he made the first of many trips to Europe. In London he learned more about printing and sampled the pleasures of the large, bustling capital city.

Two years after his return to Philadelphia in 1726, Franklin bought the newspaper called the *Pennsylvania Gazette*. By 1730 he had married Deborah. Their marriage was a long and happy one, and they had three children. She died in 1774.

Left, a London coffee-house in about 1700. Coffeehouses were important centers of political discussion.

Right, Franklin at two stages in his life: arriving poor and hungry in Philadelphia, and thriving as a newspaper owner.

9

The Junto

In 1727 Franklin and other Philadelphia leaders and businesspeople formed a group called the Junto. They organized many projects for the good of their city and its people. These included a library, a hospital, a college (later to become the University of Pennsylvania), and also America's first fire brigade.

Franklin wearing the uniform of the Union Fire Company.

Engraving of the mid-1600s showing a large block of soap being cut into pieces.

A Successful Book

In 1732 Franklin published the first edition of his *Poor Richard's Almanac*. This was a yearly book filled with varied facts and figures. Franklin wrote many mottos, sayings, and homespun truths. Some of these were taken from his wide experience of reading – he had taught himself to understand several foreign languages.

One of the **almanac**'s best-known sayings was: "Early to bed, early to rise, makes a man healthy, wealthy and wise." Most of the sayings were about the benefits of work, honesty, and simple decency.

The almanac became a huge best-seller. Most years it sold 10,000 copies. By now Franklin had established a variety of business interests, including book shops, printing companies, and also publishers. He would be wealthy for life. And so, in 1748, he decided to retire from active business and take up a new and completely different career – as a scientist.

A page from the 1733 edition of Franklin's almanac.

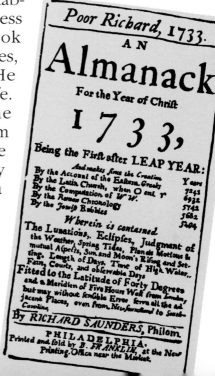

Chapter Three
From Stoves to Spectacles

Throughout his life, Benjamin Franklin had great curiosity about the world around him. He wanted to know how things worked and why. He was also able to think clearly about problems and devise tests and experiments to find the answer. His experiments were uncomplicated and used very simple homemade equipment. He was skilled with his hands, partly as a result of his training with printing machines.

Pure and Applied Research

Franklin was one of the first people to show that "pure research" could also have useful results. Pure scientific research is carried out to gain knowledge for its own sake. It differs from applied research, which is carried out by people such as inventors. They are trying to produce something which can be applied, or put to practical use.

Franklin carried out pure research, mainly in electricity (see page 15). But he also envisioned many useful applications for the results of all his experiments.

A portrait of Franklin as a prosperous businessman in his middle age.

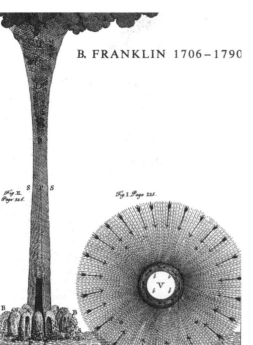

B. FRANKLIN 1706–1790

Left, a diagram showing Franklin's ideas on high and low atmospheric pressure.

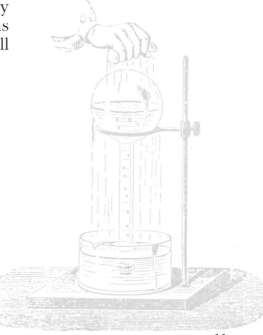

Keep the Fires Burning

Until the 18th century, log fires were very inefficient. They were very smoky and much of their heat was lost up through the chimney.

Franklin also carried out applied research. One of his first scientific achievements was an invention to meet an important need.

In 18th-century North America, the main source of heat in the home was an open wood fire. The smoke from thousands of fires made Philadelphia very gloomy and sooty. There was also the real danger that sparks flying out of the chimneys might set the wooden houses on fire.

Franklin observed that most of the heat from an open log fire went straight up the chimney. He wondered if some of this lost heat could be transferred to the room. Less fuel would then be needed to warm the room, reducing the homeowner's costs.

More Heat, Less Fuel

The result of his work was the "Pennsylvania fireplace" or "Franklin stove," which he designed in 1740. It soon became popular all over North America and also in Europe.

The log fire was enclosed in a large hoodlike structure, open at the front so the flames could be seen. Just behind the burning logs was an airbox, around which the smoke passed before it went up the chimney and out into the open.

Air was drawn into the airbox from below the floor and was heated as it passed by the fire. This heated air left the airbox through holes in the side of the fireplace and warmed the room. This harnessed the heat that would normally have been lost up the chimney. Also, the fire burned more steadily in a controlled way so fewer sparks flew out of the chimney, which made it much safer.

For the Benefit of All

The Pennsylvania authorities were very pleased. They offered Franklin the **patent** for his design, which meant he could earn money for every Pennsylvania fireplace made. But he refused, saying that he was glad to be able to serve others.

He was also aware that if people wasted wood, they would have to cut down more trees. He wrote in his reply: "Since fuel (wood) is become so expensive, ... any new proposal for saving the wood may at least be worth consideration."

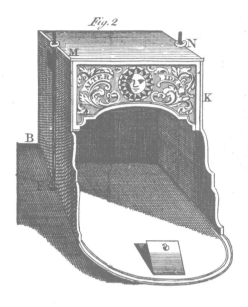

An engraving of a "Franklin stove," an early radiator.

European settlers in North America chopping down trees for firewood and construction.

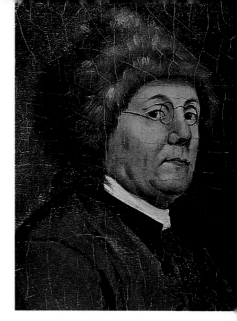

Benjamin Franklin wearing a pair of his bifocals in the 1780s.

The Armonica

Ben Franklin's talents even extended to making music. In the 1760s he invented an instrument called the Armonica. Glass bowls were fixed to a long, horizontal spindle that turned them around through a trough of water. Each bowl was a different size, for a different note. As the bowls turned, the player's fingertips touched the rims to produce the delicate humming notes. Mozart and Beethoven both wrote music for this new instrument.

Two Pairs for One

Even near the end of his life, while living in France, Franklin was still inventing gadgets. Spectacles with glass lenses had been in use for many years. But due to the effects of age on the eyes, some older people needed two pairs. One had **convex** lenses for reading and close work. The other had less convex lenses for looking at faraway objects.

In 1784 Franklin hit upon the idea of having both types of lenses in the same frame. We now call them bifocal glasses.

Ideas and Gadgets

Franklin invented dozens of other gadgets, including a fan that he could operate with his feet to keep himself cool while reading. He was also a never-ending source of sensible ideas. In the same year that he invented bifocals, he was also the first person to suggest changing the clocks between winter and summer. Franklin wanted people to get the most benefit from the hours of daylight so that they could have "the pure light of the Sun for nothing."

Wolfgang Amadeus Mozart (1756-1791)

Chapter Four
The Electrical Fluid

Benjamin Franklin's most famous scientific work was in the area of electrostatics, or static electricity – electricity that is usually not moving, but is still or stationary.

Until the end of the 18th century, people only knew about static electricity. They did not know about moving or flowing electricity – that is, the electric current so familar today. Batteries (electrical cells) and generators, which make electric current, had not been invented.

Electricity and Magnetism

For centuries, electricity had been confused with **magnetism**. In ancient Greece, the mathematician Thales of Miletus (c. 624-546 B.C.) described rubbing a piece of **amber** with fur or wool. It would then pull towards it, or attract, light objects such as feathers. Indeed, the term *electricity* comes from "electron," the Greek name for amber.

These two invisible attracting forces, magnetism and electricity, were thought to be the same until about the 17th century.

A bust of the Greek scientist and mathematician Thales of Miletus (c. 624-546 B.C.).

Below left, a sample of a magnetic mineral called magnetite or lodestone.

Below right, a fossilized fly about 30 million years old trapped in a piece of amber.

A portrait of William Gilbert, scientist and physician to Queen Elizabeth I.

Pioneers of Electrostatics

Many scientists had worked with static electricity. They tested different ways of making it and tried its effects on different substances – including their own bodies!

• William Gilbert (1544-1603) was an English scientist and physician to Queen Elizabeth I. He was one of the first people to distinguish between magnetism and electricity, calling those substances that behaved like amber "electric."

• Otto von Guericke (1602-1686), the German scientist, built a machine for producing static electricity – what we would call an electrostatic generator. It was a large ball of sulphur in a glass globe that was turned by handle. When the globe was rubbed with a cloth, it became charged with static electricity.

• Stephen Gray (1666-1736), an English physicist, tested many different substances to see if they carried electricity. In 1729 he distinguished between **conductors**, which could carry or conduct electricity, and **insulators**, which would not.

Otto von Guericke's experiment of 1670 with electrical repulsion.

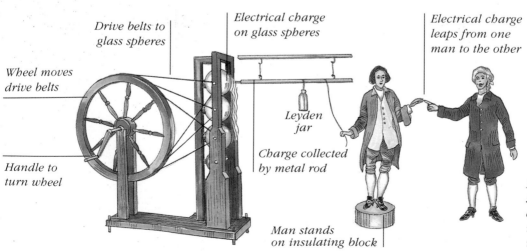

Wheel moves drive belts

Handle to turn wheel

Drive belts to glass spheres

Electrical charge on glass spheres

Electrical charge leaps from one man to the other

Leyden jar

Charge collected by metal rod

Man stands on insulating block

Diagram showing a static electricity machine of the mid-1700s.

The "Electrical Fluid"

Gradually, scientists began to distinguish between static electricity and magnetism. By Franklin's day, there were toys, tricks, and public displays that used static electricity as a form of entertainment. They produced spectacular, large sparks and made people jump with electric shocks.

People called this mysterious, unseen force "electrical fluid." They imagined it might be like a liquid. It seemed that it was usually static or stationary in the object. But given the right conditions, it could jump or move from one object to another. In damp conditions, the electrical fluid seemed to leak away into the air as though drying out or **evaporating**, similar to a fluid such as water.

Storing Static

In 1745, in Germany, a scientist named Ewald von Kleist (c. 1700-1748) tried to prevent the electrical fluid from evaporating by storing it in a sealed jar containing water. He succeeded, the static electricity remaining in the jar for many hours. It became known as the Leyden jar after being used and perfected at the University of Leyden in Holland.

The Leyden Jar

The Leyden jar was an important development in people's knowledge of electricity. It consisted of a glass jar with a cork stopper. It had an outer covering made of metal and contained water. The inside surface of the jar was charged (electrified) by touching a brass rod on an electrostatic generator. The static electricity then passed down the rod to the water inside the jar, where it stayed until drawn off by touching the metal rod again.

Three Men in a Row

In one of Franklin's famous experiments, three men stood near each other. The first two stood on wax sheets, to prevent any electricity from leaking into the ground. Person A first electrified a glass tube by rubbing it with silk. Person B put his finger near the tube, and a small spark leaped across the gap. He then put his finger near the finger of Person C, and another spark jumped across. The electricity was passed from one person to another, until it leaked from Person C (who wasn't on a wax sheet) into the ground.

A New Interest

In 1746, just before his retirement from business, Benjamin Franklin went on a trip to his birthplace, Boston. He saw a demonstration of electrical fluid and its effects, including shocks and sparks. At once he became interested and wrote to his colleague Peter Collinson in London. Collinson was an agent for the Philadelphia Library and also a member of the **Royal Society**. He sent Franklin books and electrical equipment, and Franklin set to work on his experiments.

Franklin obtained an electrostatic generator, a Leyden jar, metal and glass spheres, and many other pieces of equipment. He repeated several of the standard experiments on electrical fluids. He also gave demonstrations to startled visitors, and his house became a popular meeting place.

However, as usual, Franklin wanted to find out more. So he carried out experiments with the help of friends from the Junto, including one using three people in a row (see panel left).

An engraving of Benjamin Franklin in the late 1780s. It shows him wearing his bifocal spectacles and experimenting with electricity.

Positive and Negative

As a result of his experiments, Franklin declared that there were not two kinds of electrical fluid but one. In most objects, the fluid existed in a normal or neutral amount. In some electrified objects, there was too much fluid. Others did not have enough. Franklin called these two states *positive* and *negative* – the first use of these now-common words for electricity.

Franklin also said that you could not create or make the electrical fluid. You could only move or transfer it from place to place, thereby producing electrical effects. This is another central idea in electricity, now called the **principle of conservation of charge** (see page 23).

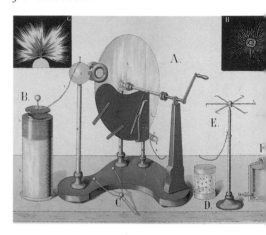

A "winter battery" to generate static electricity, with a Leyden jar attached.

More Stored Electricity

Franklin devised a better version of the Leyden jar with thin metal foil on the inside and outside. This could hold more electrical charge. He then discovered that a flat glass plate sandwiched between two sheets of lead worked just as well.

By linking several such plates together, he could store even more electricity. These were early forms of a device called a **capacitor**, now common in many electrical circuits.

Benjamin Franklin's experiments with electricity, turned into an 18th-century parlor game.

19

Chapter Five
Playing with Fire

Like other scientists of the day, Franklin also wondered if there was any connection between the sparks of electricity made in his laboratory and the gigantic bolts of lightning from thunderstorms that often set fire to and destroyed many tall buildings. He also discovered that a metal point was good at collecting the "electrical fire." Putting these two ideas together, Franklin came up with the remarkable idea of the lightning conductor.

Flying Kites

The English chemist Joseph Priestley (1733-1804) described Franklin's 1752 experiment with a kite in a thunderstorm. Franklin wanted to gather electricity from the cloud and bring it down to earth. The kite had a metal rod with a sharp point aiming upwards. This gathered electricity from the overhead thundercloud. The string, wet from the rain, conducted the electricity down. A key was tied to the kite string and

The first lightning conductor, placed on a Philadelphia house in 1752.

Joseph Priestley was a great admirer of Benjamin Franklin.

Franklin performed a number of experiments with kites in storms.

dangled near a Leyden jar. Sure enough, sparks jumped from the key to the jar, and the jar became full or charged with electricity.

A Lucky Escape

Franklin was incredibly lucky to survive this experiment. If he had encountered a real bolt of lightning, he would certainly have been killed. In fact, this happened to a Russian scientist named Georg Richmann in St. Petersburg, in 1753. He was hit on the head by a gigantic spark and died instantly.

The Franklin Rod

In 1752, Franklin fitted the first lightning conductor to the outside wall of a house. People were very suspicious at first. They thought that the tall rod pointing up to the heavens, waiting to be struck by awesome lightning, would interfere with the will of God. But gradually they accepted the idea. The new lightning conductor, which became known as the Franklin rod, soon proved its practical worth.

Georg Richmann was killed by lightning while experimenting.

This particular sort of lightning is called forked lightning.

Modern Views

How does modern science view the "electrical fluid"? The idea of a fluid has long since been replaced. Electricity of any kind exists because of the presence and movement of electrons. Electrons are one type of particle that make up atoms, the smallest complete units of matter.

In a normal atom, the electrons go around a central core or **nucleus**, like planets orbiting the sun. Each electron is negative – that is, it has a negative electrical charge. This charge is balanced by a corresponding positive charge in the nucleus.

However, the energy from rubbing and **friction** can cause electrons to become separated from the rest

English chemist John Dalton (1766-1844) was the father of modern atomic theory.

This diagram shows the modern view of an atom, with electrons spinning around the nucleus.

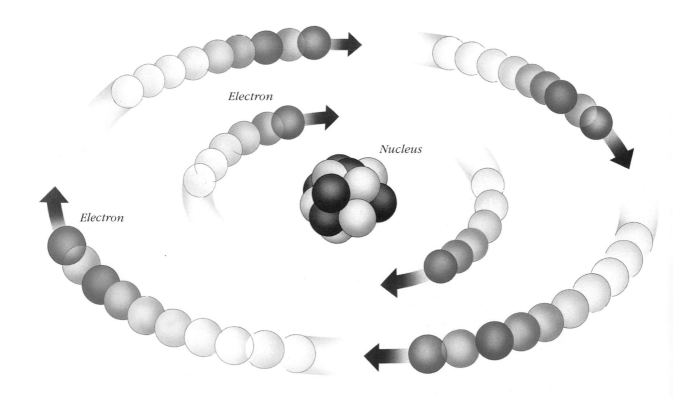

Electron

Electron

Nucleus

of the atom. They can move on their own to other objects. These free electrons represent negative charges and a flow of electricity. The object they move to gains extra electrons – it is negatively charged. The object they leave behind has a surplus of positive nuclei – it is positively charged.

So static electricity is really too many or too few electrons. As Franklin suggested, charges are not created or made. The charged parts, electrons and nuclei, are separated from each other. This is known as the principle of conservation of charge. When sparks fly or shocks happen, this represents electrons and nuclei getting back together and restoring the balance once again.

An early model of an atom was made by English physicist Joseph Thomson (1856-1940).

Static or Flowing

All electricity has the same basic form. But it behaves in different ways. Imagine this comparison between electricity and water.

A Leyden jar full of static electricity – that is, stored electric charge – could be like a huge barrel filled with water. The only way to obtain the water is to tip over the barrel. All the water comes out in an uncontrolled rush. This is like a Leyden jar giving up, or discharging, its electricity with a quick and violent spark or a sudden electric shock.

An electrical battery (cell) is more like a barrel full of water with a tap. Open the tap, and you obtain a steady, controlled flow of water – that is, an electric current.

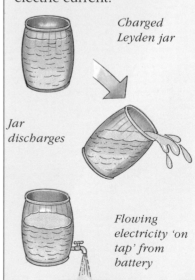

Charged Leyden jar

Jar discharges

Flowing electricity 'on tap' from battery

Chapter Six

Across the Ocean

In 1751 Franklin published his book *Experiments and Observations on Electricity, made at Philadelphia in America.* It was a major advance in physics, but it also marked the end of his main experimental work in the subject. Loaded with honors, Franklin then became internationally famous as a public leader, politician, **diplomat,** and spokesman for the emerging nation of America.

American Independence

Most of Ben Franklin's energy in later years was devoted to peace, then war, then peace again, as America decided to become a separate nation. The inhabitants of the North American colonies could not vote for their members in Parliament or influence affairs such as how much tax they paid. This created much resentment, and many colonists were determined to break with England.

In 1776 Franklin was one of the three authors of the Declaration of Independence, as America fought to become a free country. By 1781 the Revolutionary War was over, but the peace negotiations continued for another two years.

The drafting of the Declaration of Independence. Franklin is on the left in the painting.

Franklin as ambassador to France at the court of King Louis XVI. He was a great success and was invited to all the important parties.

24

The map of the Gulf Stream, drawn by Franklin in the 1770s. It shows the stream running up the coast of North America and turning east toward Europe.

The Gulf Stream

On his frequent journeys between America and Europe, Franklin's inquisitive mind was still hard at work. He knew that sailing from America to Europe took less time than going the other way, even taking into account wind speeds. In 1770 the American postal authorities asked him to investigate the reason for this, so as to help speed the mail ships.

Franklin was the first person to study and map the Gulf Stream. He described this as a vast mid-ocean "river" of warm water. It flows gently from the West Indies, up the east coast of North America, and then across the Atlantic to Europe. It was this east-bound flow of water that enabled the ships to Europe to sail faster than those going the other way.

The Final Years

Benjamin Franklin returned home to Philadelphia from Europe for the last time in 1785. He was an immensely famous and respected figure, and he helped to write the American **constitution** for his new nation. Although in his old age he suffered from a number of illnesses, he was always cheerful and curious about the world and events. He died in Philadelphia on April 17, 1790, leaving a lasting mark on the worlds of science and politics.

Benjamin Franklin's grave in Philadelphia. His death was mourned all over the country.

Chapter Seven
After Franklin

The Van der Graaff generator creates static electricity that makes the girl's hair stand up.

Only ten years after Franklin's death, Italian scientist Alessandro Volta (1745-1827) invented the electrical cell or battery. It produced a steady flow of charge, in the form of an electric current. It also opened a vast new area for scientists studying electricity – the field of electrodynamics, or "electricity on the move."

Within a few decades, other scientists such as Hans Oersted (1777-1851), Michael Faraday (1791-1867) and Joseph Henry (1797-1878) were studying dynamic electricity and inventing **electromagnets**, electric motors, and **transformers**.

Electrostatics took second place to the new science of electrodynamics. But people continued to research it, and it still had its applications. Bigger electrostatic machines were built, such as Van der Graaf generators, to make charges of millions of volts. These were used in physics research to discover the nature and composition of atoms and other particles.

Volta demonstrates his battery before the French emperor Napoleon.

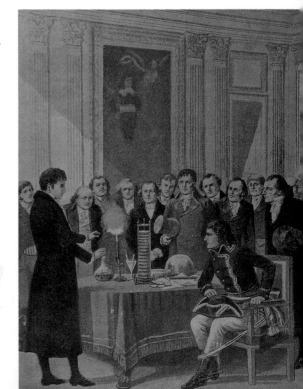

Chester Carlson (1906-1968), who invented the xerox system used today in photocopying machines.

A portrait of Benjamin Franklin in old age painted in 1789, the year before his death.

Leyden jars went through many designs and became the modern devices known as capacitors (condensers), vital to many electrical circuits. Variable capacitors with leaves or metal plates are used for tuning radios to diffcrent stations.

In 1938 an American scientist and lawyer, Chester Carlson (1906-1968), devised a machine that used electrostatic attraction to pull patterns of ink powder onto a sheet of paper. Called electrophotography, it was the basis of the **photocopier**. Electrostatics also finds many other applications today, from the spray-painting of cars and similar objects to the **filtering** of particles from dirty air.

Next time you pass a tall building such as a church and see the lightning conductor or Franklin rod, remember the remarkable man who made so many contributions to science, world history, and the lives of "ordinary folk."

The World in Franklin's Time

	1706-1725	1726-1750
Science	**1706** Benjamin Franklin born in Boston, Massachusetts **1714** Daniel Fahrenheit invents a temperature scale **1714** Spanish Academy of Science founded in Madrid **1718** Lady Mary Wortley Montagu introduces smallpox inoculation	**1727** Death of British scientist Sir Isaac Newton **1730** René de Réaumur invents his temperature scale **1736** John Harrison builds the first chronometer capable of keeping accurate time at sea
Exploration	**1709** First mass emigration of Germans to Pennsylvania **1722** Easter Island, a remote island in the Pacific, is discovered by Jakob Roggeveen	**1728** Vitus Bering first sails through the Bering Strait (named after him), between Siberia and Alaska **1732** James Oglethorpe founds the colony of Georgia **1735** French East India Company founds sugar industry in Mauritius
Politics	**1706** Defense of Charleston, South Carolina, against French and Spanish **1715** King Louis XIV of France dies after a long reign **1718** New Orleans, Louisiana, founded	**1739** War between English and Spanish in West Indies **1740** Bengal becomes an independent state under Alivardi Khan **1745** British capture Louisburg
Art	**1706** Excavations begin at Pompeii and Herculaneum in Italy **1719** Daniel Defoe writes *Robinson Crusoe* **1721** Johann Sebastian Bach composes his *Brandenburg Concertos*	**1734** Francois de Voltaire writes his *Lettres sur les Anglais* **1740** University of Pennsylvania founded **1741** George Handel composes the *Messiah*

1751-1775	1776-1800

1752 Benjamin Franklin installs the first lightning conductor

1780 Luigi Galvani makes important discoveries in electricity

1764 James Watt invents his steam condenser

1781 William Herschel first views the planet Uranus

1774 Joseph Priestley discovers oxygen

1790 Death of Benjamin Franklin

1794 First semaphore telegraph, between Paris and Lille

1766 British first occupy the Falkland Islands

1791 George Vancouver begins his exploration of north-west coast of America

1768 Captain James Cook sets out on his exploration of the South Seas

1798 French expedition to Egypt sets out

1799 Alexander Humboldt's scientific expedition to South America

1754 Outbreak of Anglo-French war in North America

1776 American Declaration of Independence

1757 Robert Clive wins the Battle of Plassey in India

1783 Treaty of Paris recognizes United States as a nation

1768 Outbreak of war between Turkey and Russia

1793 Execution of King Louis XVI of France

1753 British Museum founded

1777 Richard Sheridan writes *School for Scandal*

1764 Horace Walpole writes the *Castle of Otranto*

1782 Wolfgang Mozart writes *Elopement from the Seraglio*

1771 First edition of the *Encyclopaedia Britannica*

1800 Ludvig van Beethoven composes his *First Symphony*

1775 Pierre de Beaumarchais writes *Le Barbier de Séville*

Glossary

almanac: a record of the days, weeks, and months of the year, listing important events, anniversaries, and other information.

amber: the yellow resin (sap) of certain types of trees formed into fossils over millions of years.

apprentice: someone who is being trained by another to learn a particular craft or skill.

battery: *see* **cell.**

broadsheet: a newspaper, usually printed on one side of a large piece of paper.

capacitor: an electrical device that can store large amounts of electrical charge.

cell: in electrical work, a device containing various chemicals that produces a flow of electricity. More accurately, a single device like this is called a cell, and two or more linked together make a battery.

colony: a settlement of people in a distant country who maintain close ties with their homeland.

conductor: something, often a metal, that conducts or transmits heat or electricity from one place to another.

constitution: the fundamental principles of the government of a nation, embodied in its laws, institutions, and customs.

convex: rising into a round shape. A convex lens enables someone to see close-up, detailed work more clearly.

diplomat: someone involved in diplomacy, the art of negotiation in relations between states.

electric current: a flow of electricity through a substance, for example through a metal wire.

electromagnet: a device in which an electric current, passing through a wire coiled around a soft iron core, produces a magnetic field.

evaporate: to turn into a vapor or gas. A liquid such as water will evaporate when heated and turn into water vapor.

filter: the process of removing unwanted particles by passing them through a fine screening device.

friction: the resistance to the movement of one thing rubbed against another.

immigrant: someone who moves to a new country with the intention of settling there.

insulator: a material, often plastic or rubber, that prevents electricity or heat from being transmitted from one place to another.

magnetism: a still-mysterious force, produced by a magnet or an electric current, that can attract or repel substances at a distance.

Native Americans: the original people who inhabited the Americas before the arrival of European settlers.

nucleus: the very heart or center of something.

patent: a legal document showing that someone is the official inventor of a device or product and has the sole right to make and sell it for a certain time period.

photocopier: a machine that uses the attractive force of electric charges to transfer an image to a charged plate and then onto paper.

principle of conservation of charge: a central idea in the scientific study of electricity that states that charges are not created but are transferred.

Royal Society: the oldest scientific society in Great Britain, founded in 1660.

spectacles: in this case, a pair of viewing lenses mounted in frames with side arms. Designed to enable the wearer to see better.

transformer: an electrical device that transforms an electric current, that is, makes it stronger or weaker in terms of voltage.

Index

STEVE PARKER has written more than 40 books for children, including several in the Eyewitness series. He has a bachelor of science degree in zoology and is a member of the Zoological Society of London.